How to Analyze People

Understanding What People Are Thinking

By Erik Smith

I0425423

Table Of Contents

Free Stuff

Do you want to get notified when I have free books? Then sign up for my newsletter. I will never spam you. I will only send you valuable stuff that you can use to help you improve your life.

Sign up here - http://forms.aweber.com/form/26/1968511626.htm

Disclaimer

This document is geared towards providing exact and reliable information in regards to the topic and issue covered. The publication is sold with the idea that the publisher is not required to render accounting, officially permitted, or otherwise, qualified services. If advice is necessary, legal or professional, a practiced individual in the profession should be ordered.

- From a Declaration of Principles which was accepted and approved equally by a Committee of the American Bar Association and a Committee of Publishers and Associations.

The information provided herein is stated to be truthful and consistent, in that any liability, in terms of inattention or otherwise, by any usage or abuse of any policies, processes, or directions contained within is the solitary and utter responsibility of the recipient reader. Under no circumstances will any legal responsibility or blame be held against the publisher for any reparation, damages, or monetary loss due to the information herein, either directly or indirectly.

The information herein is offered for informational purposes solely, and is universal as so. The presentation of the information is without contract or any type of guarantee assurance.

The trademarks that are used are without any consent, and the publication of the trademark is without permission or backing by the trademark owner. All trademarks and brands within this book are for clarifying purposes only and are the owned by the owners themselves, not affiliated with this document.

Introduction

In a perfect world, all the people you encounter are perfectly honest in their dealings with you. There will be no threats of dishonesty and backstabbing, everyone will know who are the people they can truly trust. However, the world does not work that way. There are so many people these days who would repeatedly lie (often right in your face) just so they can get what they want from you. The only way you can protect yourself from these kinds of people is to beat them at their own game; you need to learn how to analyze people so you can strip away their symbolic masks and uncover the truth underneath.

In this book, you will learn the basics of analyzing people. Do keep in mind that reading people is not the same as reading minds; the former is a skill, the latter is impossible. You will learn the intricacies behind reading a person's expressions, body language, tone of voice, and other "tells" that are indicative of deception.

By the end of this book, you would have learned everything that you need to protect yourself from people who want to take advantage of you. You can also use your newfound skills to help the people who are close to you..

Thanks for downloading this book, I hope you enjoy it!

Why Do You Need to Analyze People?

Have you ever been cheated on? For instance, by your significant other when he/she told you that he/she has been totally faithful to you, and that the only reason why he/she decided to break up with you is because he/she wants to "re-discover" himself/herself, only to find out from other people that your SO has been seeing someone else on the side. Another example would be when an acquaintance approaches you with a shady business proposal, and then later finding out that you have just become a victim of a Ponzi scheme.

These are just some of the instances wherein the ability to analyze people would have been handy. If you think that you are lucky enough to not have been a victim of dishonest people then you were most likely so deceived that you did not even notice. There are so many reasons why you need to learn how to read people, and if you need a bit more convincing, then consider the following:

It will help you improve your personal relationships

Here's a familiar scenario: you come back home to see your spouse sitting alone at the dinner table. You ask him/her if there's anything wrong, and you get the common reply "No, I'm fine." This is one of the many tricky situations in all relationships, one person expects the other to read between the lines, while the other person takes the answer literally and assumes that everything is indeed "fine". Many arguments have started just because people cannot read what the other person is actually trying to say.

When you know how to read people, you can almost immediately tell what your significant other actually wants to tell you, and he/she will appreciate you for doing so. No more sleepless nights spent on the sofa for you!

It will help you bolster your career

The modern workplace is almost akin to a rough battlefield; you might find a couple of friends there, but the truth is that it is every man for him/herself. Your so-called friends would not hesitate to throw you under the bus if it meant that they can get a raise or a promotion. You really cannot trust anyone in the workplace, that is if you do not know how to read them. When you know how to read people, you will know who are actually your real friends, and who are the ones who digging for dirt that they can report to the HR.

Another way that reading people can help you get ahead in the workplace is you can use it when negotiating with your bosses. For instance, you can most likely tell if your boss is just bluffing when he told you that the company simply cannot afford giving you that raise that you know have been due for the past couple of months, or even years. When you can read the emotions of your boss, you can then counter-attack with a bluff of your own and watch him take the bait.

You can protect yourself from getting fleeced

Here's a situation that you might have experienced before: an old high school acquaintance (you were not really that close back then) out of the blue contacted you and asked how you have been. Your conversation seems very innocent enough, reminiscing about the times when you were still teenagers, and the common friends that the both of you had. Suddenly, he pulls out a binder and then immediately starts talking about a "business opportunity" that you simply should not let pass. If you did not know any better, it would seem that your "friend" really wanted to help you, but if you know how to read his intentions, you will know that he just wants to recruit your into his network marketing scheme.

You can also use people reading skills to help you get good deals. For instance, if you are in the market for a new car, then you have to deal with the sales agents. The problem here is that these sales agents are trained manipulators; they know which buttons to push to make you agree to a one-sided deal that only benefits them. When you know how to read people, you and the salesperson will be on a somewhat level playing field, which means you can get a deal that is mutually beneficial for the both of you.

You can protect yourself and the ones you love from actual harm

If you are a fan of Japanese animation or anime, then you probably are familiar about certain characters sensing the bloodlust coming from other people, and when they do they immediately spring into action before any harm comes to them. You can basically do the same thing when you know how to read people; no, you cannot sense their bloodlust or their killing intent, but you will get the next best thing.

When you can read people, even a short glance will tell you if someone means to do you harm. You can call it your intuition if you like, or you can even call it your own Spider-sense, but the truth is that you observed the person, and you saw all of the telltale signs of aggression against you. This skill is always handy; you can use it during your daily commute to and from work, you can use it while you are at work, and you can also use this while you are running errands. Keep in mind that danger lurks in every corner, so it is for your best interest if you know how to anticipate and identify it from afar.

These are only a couple of the many valid reasons why you need to learn how to analyze people. You will learn more uses for this skill the more you use it. The important thing is that you get the basic gist of it all, and that is there is nothing to lose and everything to gain just by learning this important skill.

Techniques On How to Read People

There are basically three main techniques to read people, and they are:

I. Observe the Person's Body Language

Numerous researches have proven that the spoken word only account for 7% of the actual way people communicate, however, body language accounts for 55%. it might sound surprising, but you actually get more information if you pay more attention to the other person's body language instead of focusing on what he is saying (although that is important as well). Shoulder shrugs, crossed legs, fidgeting fingers, raised eyebrows, and many other cues can tell you more about a person than what he/she is actually telling you.

Here are some of the said body language cues that you need to look out for when you want to analyze people:

1. The person's overall appearance

"Clothes maketh the man", this quote from William Shakespeare's Hamlet still holds true in today's modern world. The clothes is the first thing that people will notice when they meet other people for the first time, and the way they dress and carry themselves actually do tell a lot about their personality. So, when you first meet someone, check out his clothes and how he wears them.

Is the person wearing a power suit and a pair of well-kept shoes? This might be an indication that the person is ambitious. Is he wearing a pair of jeans and a cotton t-shirt? This means that the person is casual and values comfort over everything else. Is the person wearing a shirt with a plunging neckline, showing quite a lot of cleavage, and wearing a pendant that draws the eyes to the chest? This is a clear sign of seduction.

2. Observe the person's posture and how he carries himself

The way a person carries him/herself can also tell a lot about his personality. You can even tell if the person is being truthful or not. For instance, a person who has his chest puffed out and holding his chin real high may seem confident, but he is actually over-exaggerating to compensate for his complete lack of confidence. A truly confident person walks with his head held high, but not so much that he seems to look down on others.

Other posture cues include, walking with the head pointing down is a sign of low self-esteem, and so is walking with an exaggerated swagger, however the second one is also indicative of a big, yet fragile ego.

3. Keep an eye out for any movement

Subtle gestures and movements might seem inconsequential, but they actually betray quite a lot of what the person is thinking about. These small movements are so miniscule that they are done almost unconsciously, which is why they make for great "tells". For instance:

Leaning direction and distance – People in general tend to lean toward the things that they like, and lean away from the things that they dislike. Keep this in mind when talking to another person, notice if he/she is leaning towards you, or if the person would almost fall out of his/her chair due to leaning away from you.

Crossed arms and legs – These body positions suggest defensiveness, self-protection, and maybe even anger. When people cross their legs, they would usually point their feet towards the person they feel most comfortable with. If the person's feet is pointing towards the nearest exit, it is a sign of extreme apprehension and a clear want to escape; take this as a cue to calm the person down if you want to get even more information.

Hiding the hands – When a person places his hands on his lap, in his pockets, or put them where you cannot see them then there is a good chance that the person is hiding something from you. You should be wary of these people as you can never really tell where their loyalties lie.

Lip biting and cuticle picking – Lip biting, cuticle picking, and other fidgeting movements mean that the person is under a lot of stress and is trying their hardest to calm themselves down.

4. Check Their Facial Expressions

Humans are one of the very few creatures on Earth that can show their emotions through their facial expressions. This is ingrained into human DNA that it is almost impossible to remove all traces of emotions from their faces. Look for telltale cues that are almost impossible to suppress, like crow's feet at the sides of the eyes signify genuine joy and happiness, so when a person smiles at you, but there are no crow's feet (or even hints of them) appearing around his eyes, that is an insincere smile.

II. Trusting Your Intuition

Aside from a person's body and actual words, there is another way you can tune into what he is actually feeling, and that is through your intuition. Trusting your intuition means going with your gut feel, despite of what your brain is telling you. Your intuition is composed of all the non-verbal cues that you perceived, these are the things that your gut tells you must be the truth, and they might not necessarily be logical at first, but for you it just feels right.

To truly understand a person, you have to know who the person is, and not just look at his/her outer trappings. Your intuition will let you see deeper into someone's personality to reveal a rich story underneath.

Here are some of the Intuitive Cues that you need to keep an eye out for:

1. Believe your gut feelings

It is actually important that you at least consider what your gut is telling you, especially when you are meeting someone for the first time. Your gut feel is a visceral reaction that happens a bit before your brain actually starts to think in earnest. Basically, it tells you whether you are at ease or not; it's a primal reaction that helped prehistoric humans to steer clear of dangerous situations. Your gut, illogical as it might sound, tells you whether you can trust someone or not.

2. Feel your goosebumps

Goosebumps are yet another primal reaction passed down from the prehistoric humans. Goosebumps usually occur when you suddenly feel cold, this is because your muscles are involuntarily reacting to keep you warm. Goosebumps also appear when you suddenly feel threatened, this time your muscles are tensing up in anticipation of your flight or flight response. So when you feel goosebumps appearing on your forearm the moment you first meet someone, it might be telling you something important.

3. Deja vu

In the first Matrix movie, Morpheus told his crew to scramble when Neo experienced deja vu, this is actually also applicable in real life. Although experiencing deja vu is not actually the Matrix overcorrecting itself (or it might be) it is still a gut feeling that you need to give some serious consideration to.

4. Take flashes of insight seriously

During the course of a conversation, there is a chance that you will experience a "eureka moment" or a flash of insight about the person you're talking with. You need to be alert every time you are talking with someone because these eureka moments are quite fleeting and might be gone in a flash.

5. Be on the lookout for intuitive empathy

Are there times when you suddenly felt as if you also feel other people's pain and emotions? This is called intuitive empathy, which is an intense form of empathy. When you are reading people, take notice when you are feeling something that you did not feel before. For instance, your back suddenly hurt when talking to another person, but your back was perfectly fine earlier.

III. Sensing Emotional Energy

Note: this technique borders on the fantastic, so if you are a bit of a skeptic, you can skip this one and focus on the first two instead.

This is a more spiritual based technique on reading people. Depending on your mood, the "vibe" that you give off will also change, mainly because

8

emotions are expressions of your energy, and you can sense all of these using your intuition. For instance, some people make you feel good whenever you are with them, and there are others who make you feel emotionally and physically drained just after a couple of minutes talking with them.

This subtle energy put out by your body is invisible, but you can feel it a couple of inches to a couple of feet from the surface of your body. In Chinese medicine, this energy is called "chi" and it is essential for your health.

To read a person's emotional energy, follow these tips:

1. Feel other people's presence

The presence is the overall energy that all people naturally emit. This is not necessarily related to their words or behavior, it is more like an emotional aura that surrounds them. When reading people, take note of the following: do they have a friendly presence that you feel attracted to? Or are you getting a sick feeling in your stomach that somewhat tells you to back away?

2. Look into their eyes

A person's eyes actually transmit a form of energy, similar to how the brain sends an electromagnetic signal that surrounds the entire body. This is why it is important to observe a person's eyes when you observe them. You can actually tell of a person is caring, mean, angry, happy, and a vast array of other emotions just by looking into his/her eyes. You can also determine if there is another person who's at home in their eyes, which is indicative of a capacity for intimacy, or do their eyes look like they are hiding something or if they are guarding something.

3. Physical transmissions

Just like an electrical current, people share emotional energy through physical contact. This is the reason why some people's handshakes feel warm and confident, and other's feel off-putting and somewhat creeps you out. For instance, hands that are cold and clammy are indicative of anxiety and stress, while limp hands signal fear of commitment and/or timidness.

4. Verbal cues

The tone and volume of a person's voice can actually tell a lot about his/her current emotional status. When observing/reading another person, take note of how their voice makes you feel; is the other person's voice feel soothing, or is it whiny, creepy, abrasive, or gives you a feeling of dread.

You can choose to use any one, or a combination of all these techniques to read people. In the following chapter, you will actually learn how to use these techniques in a practical manner.

Putting Your Skills to the Test

Now that you have learned the techniques, it is time that you learn how to put them to use. Here are the actual steps that you need to take if you want to make a complete analysis of a person, and get as many details out of them as possible.

I. Establish a baseline

Different people display different quirks and behavioral patterns. For instance, some people would often clear their throats, stare at the floor while talking with others, cross their arms, and all sorts of behaviors. At first, you might not notice when they do them, and if you do, you don't give them much importance.

People display these kinds of behaviors due to different reasons. There is a chance that these are just innocent mannerisms, but there is also an equal chance that these behaviors are because of anger, fear, deception, or just plain nervousness.

1. Know the Person Thoroughly

You need to actually know a person fairly well enough to distinguish what their habits and mannerisms are, and which of their actions are "tells".

Base your opinions on at least a couple of encounters, do not draw conclusions from just one chance meeting. People might not act or speak the same way during conversations, their behavior will depend on the situation.

For instance, you might have a friend who fidgets a lot, which is not necessarily a sign of lying or nervousness. However, if you were to meet him for the first time in the streets, your gut feeling will tell you that he is nervous and anxious, which is not actually true.

Take notice of other people's habits. Do they usually maintain eye contact during conversations? How can you tell if the person is busy and cannot be disturbed? Knowing about these common habits of the person will give you a good baseline from which you can base your comparisons to.

2. Ask Open-ended Questions

Reading another person means you are both watching and listening to his/her reactions. It will not do you any good to try steering the conversation towards the direction you like, it is much better that you ask your questions, and then sit back and watch as your mark spills the beans. The best questions to ask in this case are open-ended ones, meaning they could not be answered using yes or no; these questions allow the other person to talk more.

It is best that you also ask questions that are on-point. Oftentimes, when you ask about general things, like "how's your family?" you might get a rambling speech on how unfair the world is right now; you might get some tidbits here and there, but you will not be getting anything useful. On the other hand, asking "What book are you reading now?" you can actually gather a lot more information and you do not have to filter out the senseless rabble.

3. Check Against the Baseline for Inconsistencies

Once you have gathered enough information, you can start comparing them to the baseline that you established earlier. Once you have gathered enough information about the person and how he/she normally acts, keep an eye out for anything that sticks out like a sore thumb.

However, if something does not add up, you think, ask why, at least initially. The person might simply be exhausted, or just had a rough day in general. Do not automatically assume that because you saw something odd in the person's behavior, that it is already a "tell".

4. Cluster Your Tells

Just noticing a single clue is not enough to conclude anything. The person could be leaning away from you because his/her chair is a bit uncomfortable. If you will be relying heavily on non-verbal cues, it is best to have at least three or four signs before making any assumptions. A single gesture does not mean anything, but if it is accompanied by three or more then you need to take notice.

For instance, if the person is leaning away from you, and he/she is shuffling his/her feet, he/she is talking a bit louder than usual, and would constantly clear his/her throat, then you can start conjecturing.

Try to take cues from different parts of the person's body; take cues from the person's voice, body, facial expressions, hand gestures, etc. When you get at least one tell from each, you can proceed with caution. On the other hand, if you are still unclear about the cue, or if you cannot find other tells, just ask.

5. Know Your Own Weaknesses

You are just a regular human being, and as such you are not immune to making mistakes. Whenever you see something you think is pretty, chances are that you will like it. If you see someone wearing a fine Italian suit, odds are that you will not have any trouble trusting the person. However, should you like something because it is pretty? Should you trust a person because he is well-dressed? Not necessarily.

For instance, most people think that drunk or stoned people, or homeless people were more likely to stalk them in a dark alley. However, the truth is that psychopaths are usually charming, well-dressed, and more or less looks like a normal person; someone you will not suspect to be someone to do anything evil. Although it is virtually impossible to control your subconscious from judging a person by his/her appearance, you can be aware when your brain is doing it.

II. Reading the Person's Body Language

As mentioned earlier, non-verbal cues can tell you more about what the person is actually thinking than what his/her words say. So you need to learn how to decipher these subtle physical cues as accurately as you can.

1. Take note of how they are holding themselves

You can really tell a lot about a person based on how comfortable they feel. The way they carry themselves is reflective of the topic being discussed, or it could be due to some interpersonal issues they might have. To give you some ideas, here some tips on how to gauge a person's comfort level:

Comfortable body language

- Leaning forward

- Arms relaxed and hanging at their sides

- Constant eye contact, but not overly exaggerated

- Unforced smiles

Uncomfortable body language

- Leaning away

- Arms and/or legs crossed

- Nervous/irritated fidgeting; tapping of the fingers, shaking the leg, etc.

- Looking away sometimes when talking

2. Check out their facial expressions

You need to keep out for the other person's facial expressions, especially the fleeting ones. Keep an open eye out for very subtle movements of the mouth that give away what the person is actually feeling. For instance, if a person smiles at you, but you notice a faint twitch, there is a chance that the person is thinking of something negative about you.

Anything clenched, even if only for a moment, can be taken as a sign. Furrowed brows, tensed jaws, gritting/gnashing of teeth, can be taken as signs of anxiety. In addition, if they close their eyes longer than the average blink, he/she might be taking a moment to get a grip on their current situation. This is a common indicator that a person is losing control of their situation, and they are thinking of ways to fix it, or they might be resigning themselves to their fate.

3. See if they will initiate physical contact

If the person who is usually very touchy-feely suddenly does not feel like greeting you with the usual hug, it might mean that he/she feels a bit of tension or apprehension towards you.

A weak handshake, on the other hand (no pun intended), is indicative of nervousness or being uncertain.

Touching, however, is a hard signal to really decipher since everyone has different ideas of personal space. This means that just because a person wraps his arms around your shoulder it automatically means you gained his/her trust, it could still mean that you are not within the person's inner circle yet. To really gauge how must a person trusts you, monitor how they behave when they are with other people.

4. Do they keep their distance?

Check if the other person keeps his/her distance from you. The distance a person is away from you will provide you with some insight on what they are thinking. For instance, if a person keeps his distance from you it might mean that he/she is afraid of being intimate, or feels vulnerable; it could also mean that the person is in a hurry, which is why clustering signals together is important.

There are also instances wherein the person is uncomfortable of being in close proximity from another person at all times. This means that even if a person keeps his/her distance from you, it does not necessarily mean what you think it means. This goes both ways, there are some people who have no understanding of personal space, so if they seem touchy-feely to you, they might not even be aware that they are.

5. Take the person's culture into consideration

The kind of culture a person grew up in will reflect in their behavior as an adult. For instance, in some countries, people have no problem with hugging and giving each other kisses on the cheek as a greeting to each other. You need to take these kinds of things into consideration when establishing a person's behavioral baseline.

III. Listening for Vocal Cues

When you are listening to what a person is telling you, do not just hang on every word, you also need to observe how the said words were delivered.

1. Listen to the tone of voice

The tone of a person's voice can tell you what he/she is feeling at the moment. Keep your ears open for any inconsistencies, like sounding happy and angry at the same time; this might mean that the person is hiding something from you.

You also need to take into consideration how loud the person is speaking. Compare if they are talking louder or softer than usual.

Is the person hedging by saying "umm", "like uhm"? There is a chance that the person is nervously lying to you, and he/she is still thinking of what to say, and mumbling is their way to buy themselves some more time for an answer.

Is the person's tone expressing what they are outwardly feeling? Does the other person sound angry, or maybe even sarcastic? If this is the case, the person might need to address their situation. Again, you need to consider other visual clues in addition to the ones you took notice of.

2. How long are the person's answers

If the person's answers seem short and rushed, it could mean that the person is frustrated, or is preoccupied with other, more important things. Now, if the person seems really into talking with you, continue asking your questions.

3. Take note of their choice of words

No one just blurts out words without thinking, there is always a thought process behind the things that people say. For instance, when someone tells you, "So, you bought another Ford?" The person's use of "another" seems to tell you that "Wasn't your last car a Ford? It did nothing else but break down on you, and still you bought another one?"

Now that you know all of the important things on how to read a person, go ahead and practice your skills.

Extra: How to Spot a Liar

Probably the reason why you want to learn how to read people is because you are tired of always getting taken advantage of by liars. So, to help you become a human lie detector, aside from the techniques you learned earlier, here are some of the most common "tells" that are displayed by pathological liars.

Note: Again, do not take each individual tell as conclusive evidence, remember to work with clusters.

• Take notice when the person's tone of voice suddenly changes, or if they suddenly display odd body language. For instance, if your spouse would usually hug and touch you a lot, but all of a sudden stops when you ask about a certain thing, there's a chance that your spouse is lying to you.

• Looking to the side or not making eye contact is not necessarily indicative of lying. Researchers are yet to find any relation between establishing eye contact and telling lies. There are some people who can tell you a bold-faced lie while still looking at your face; you will actually feel guilty doubting them because you feel they are really sincere.

• Take note when they start refraining from using "I". Researchers have discovered that liars would like to distance themselves from their lies as much as possible. Instead, they would start speaking about themselves in the third person. For instance, "Who's the guy who likes American football? This guy, right here!"

• Take notice when the person's story seems too detailed and elaborate. Some liars would think of a water-tight story and rehearse it several times before actually talking with someone. So watch out for stories that seem too well-polished for regular chats.

• Look into the person's eyes. One thing that liars do unconsciously is that their pupils dilate when they are telling a lie, this is an action that you really cannot train against. This is also the reason why many professional poker players wear sunglasses during indoor events.

Conclusion

I'd like to thank you and congratulate you for transiting my lines from start to finish.

I hope this book was able to help you to read and understand people better.

The next step is to take what you learned from this book into the real world. With practice you will be reading people without even thinking about it. You will no longer be an easy target for con men, and other unscrupulous individuals.

Free Stuff

Do you want to get notified when I have free books? Then sign up for my newsletter. I will never spam you. I will only send you valuable stuff that you can use to help you improve your life.

Sign up here - http://forms.aweber.com/form/26/1968511626.htm